Port Lincoln's *Bartolomeo (Bob) Puglisi*
Celebrating 50 Years of Prawn Fishing in South Australia

Bartolomeo (Bob) Puglisi has been in the fishing industry 63 years. He started working as a crew member on a fish trawler at 12½ years old in 1954, but even then had been fishing for years. He worked with his brothers in Ulladulla on the New South Wales coast, where many Puglisi families lived. The heads of these families were nearly all fishermen who had been brought out from Lipari, an island off Sicily, by his father Joe Puglisi.

In late 1967 Bob attempted to sail his small fishing vessel, the *Angelina Star*, from Ballina near the Queensland border to Port Lincoln in South Australia but was foiled by horrific weather and tried again. He was 25 years old and had been prawning for many years. He heard that in Port Lincoln fishermen wanted to fish for prawns, but had little knowledge of what to do. Beginning early in 1968, Bob brought in his first catch off Cowell. The rest is history, the history of the prawn fishing industry in South Australia. Still today Bob owns and operates two 22 metre prawn freezer vessels.

Port Lincoln's *Bartolomeo (Bob) Puglisi*

Celebrating
50 Years of
Prawn Fishing
in
South Australia

As told to

Musharella Puglisi and

Rhondda Harris

Wakefield Press

Wakefield Press
16 Rose Street
Mile End
South Australia 5031
www.wakefieldpress.com.au

First published 2017
Reprinted 2018

Printed and bound by Finsbury Green, Adelaide, South Australia

ISBN 978 1 74305 517 5

A catalogue record for this
book is available from the
National Library of Australia

To my much-loved family and for others interested in my story

14 years old 16 years old 21 years old 23 years old

My early life

Better off with Daisey

Out on my own

Meeting Jenny

Two attempts to get to South Australia

Early days in Port Lincoln – the beginnings of a prawn industry

Australian Bight Fisheries – expansion on the world market

Tragedy at home

Tuna farming – an exciting new venture for Port Lincoln

Meeting Musharella

Other ventures

Reflections

My early life

When I was two years and three days old my Mum Nina Puglisi (Lavalle) passed away and that was my Dad's second wife. We lived in Ulladulla, on the New South Wales coast, and the first memories I have are of going through a track at the back of my Grandma Puglisi's home to my Aunty Pina Costa's home carrying a basket with all I owned. Aunty Pina was my mother's sister. I went backwards and forwards as no one wanted me.

My sister Carmel (Daisey) and my two brothers, Joe and Tory, had been sent away to college in Sydney as no one wanted to look after them either. Daisey was eight, Joe was six, and Tory five. When holidays came they had to stay at school as no one came to pick them up. I was too young to go to college and there was no one for me.

Opposite: Angelina and *Beauie-J* in Port Lincoln marina, South Australia. I still operate these two beautiful boats, the remaining two of many I have owned and looked after over the years. They are now as good as they could possibly be and this makes me very proud. The smaller boats, *Maya* and *Carmel*, belong to my son Andrew now.

I know now that Grandma Puglisi had a lot on her plate. Her point was that she was looking after enough kids already and wanted someone else in the family, like someone on my mother's side, to do something. She still had two of her own children at home plus she was looking after Dad's first wife's children, the three older girls and Mick, from when their own mother had died. Josie, Mary, Nolly and Mick hadn't lived much with my mother – they didn't get along with her at all, so Grandma was the one. There were lots of reasons, Mick was very young when his Mum died so Grandma just brought him up, and with the older girls it would have been a lot for my Mum to do but it was mostly just that they were teenage kids at the time. It was hard for teenagers in an Italian community – everyone thought they could tell them what to do. Ulladulla was such a small town in those days with all the relatives knowing what you were doing. The toilets were outside the houses and you couldn't even go to the toilet without someone knowing. Mick says in his book* that his older sisters thought my mother was really strict, I don't know, I was far too young, but anyway Grandma looked after them.

I was three when World War 2 ended. From what I have been told, it was really a difficult time for all the Italian families. My father had come to Australia over 20 years earlier and in that time had brought out many

* Puglisi, Michael, *Harvesting the Sea: the story of the Puglisi family, fishing pioneers*, 2008

Opposite: My father Guiseppe (Joe) Puglisi, my mother Nina Puglisi, my brothers Joe and Tory, my sister Daisey and myself, circa 1943, at Ulladulla, New South Wales.

of the relatives and family friends. They had come from Lipari, an island off Sicily, and in Lipari they ate only fish, no other meat. They could not grow vegetables as there was no water on the island, water was brought to the island by ship. The women cooked using part fresh water, part sea water, rather than having water and adding the salt, it was not a problem for them to do that. Here in Australia they had all sorts of meat, productive gardens and of course most of the men were still fishermen.

Now the government turned suspicious about the Italians and wouldn't allow them to fish, in fact they were not allowed to go near the water. The Government especially didn't want them near Sydney Harbour and able to communicate with any passing ships. It was a big shock. All the families were naturalised and were that proud to be here but they were kept an eye on, so it was a bad feeling. They were not even permitted to keep their boats for later as the boats were needed for the war. A lot of my relatives sold their boats to the Americans, who paid a lot of dollars, and then they had money to live on. The Australian government did not pay as much, about £1,000 less each boat, but did promise to give back any boats that were left after the war, and in the same condition. So Dad sold his two boats to the Australian Navy at a lesser price.

Not being allowed to fish he established a massive garden so they could eat. His block of land was a big one, all the way from South Street to the water, next to the camping ground in Ulladulla. Some of the relatives were interned by the government but the navy got my Dad to do special work for them. His ability was that he could take a boat at night from wherever it was built and sail without any light, right along the coast. He was so familiar with the coast. He would take the boats to Garden Island where the government put in the engines to get them ready for use in New Guinea. When he wasn't doing that he had to stay on his block, he had to stay there until he got another call. After a while they let him have a job in the ship-yard at Ulladulla, building small ships to go into New Guinea to take supplies and rescue people there. All the boats the family had sold had been used for this too. Micky, my half brother, and Nolly my half sister did a lot of research about this for Mick's book. I am very proud of Micky for writing that book.

Not long after my mother died my father got hooked up with the woman next door, which caused big problems in the Lavalle family on my mother's side. It was considered a disrespect issue within the Italian community. Dad's father didn't like it much either but it was mainly the Lavalle's. The Lavalles' were all big guys and Dad had helped them all get fishing jobs, but they certainly were not impressed with him now. I was about five when my Dad and the woman next door moved to Kiama and got married. They moved there to get away from everything and so as not to cause a major problem in the town.

The war was over by then and though one of his boats had been lost in the war, the navy returned the other, the *St Michele*, the larger of the two. It was in poor condition and it cost my father as much to rebuild as to buy a new boat. He did remind the navy of their promise but was told the country was in such bad shape that they could not help. He did have his big boat again though, and he started to work it out of Kiama.

I can remember going to school in Kiama, and that I struggled – I didn't attend very much, plus I was dyslexic, I found this out later. The teacher (a nun) had five classes, with children of all different ages, in the one room, so she didn't have time for any of the kids, especially a kid like me. The school was next to the beach and there were girls from our class, young ladies, with their boyfriends on the beach on the weekend. The nun spent a lot of time lecturing those girls Monday then start again on Friday. She enjoyed that more than teaching us. It was a hard job she had – not that I am defending her in any way or thinking she was a nice person – but there wasn't a lot of time to teach us kids. It was difficult for me all the time at school, it really was, and it still is hard to do some things. It is so important to have an education so it doesn't have to be hard like this. I have always found that I have to put three times as much effort in as I can see others doing. I am very good with numbers though – at school the only subject I was good at was numbers – numbers and history.

Our step mother beat us, not so much me, as I was younger, but my brothers Joe and Tory got it all the time. She would dress up to give us a thrashing and wet the leather strap. I remember one time some older ladies in the town called the police and the cops came to the house. She was a very, very, very cruel woman and we were scared to breathe when she went off her rocker. My Dad knew about what she did, the boys always told him, but his attitude was 'she's feeding you and washing your clothes, so what are you complaining about'.

My strongest memory, the one that really sticks in my mind the most, was in 1950. I know the year because I was eight years old. I was living in Kiama when I was led to the front gate by my step mother with my older brother Tory, who was 11 years old. We were given a train fare to Sydney and I was told at the gate 'never come back'. My sister Daisey wasn't with us, she was already in Sydney with my other grandmother (Lavalle), so it was only Tory and me. Joe must have been away fishing with Dad, he would have been twelve at the time. My father Joe Puglisi was always fishing. I think he was glad to be away. He looked after us though – I remember once Joe was hit in the eye at school with a stone and Dad went there and agreed for the doctor to try out a very new drug called penicillin. Joe always had trouble with that eye, it never looked quite right, but he retained that eye until he was 65.

Woolloomooloo in Sydney, where my grandmother lived, was a rough place in those days. It was where Jimmy Carruthers lived, the one who became a boxer. My grandmother sent me to school there and most of the kids in my class were real villains. They would get dragged off to reform school for a week or so, then come back and tell us stories of what they had got up to and how they were treated. There was a teacher we had who read to us from a book at the end of each day. I remember the name, 'Boy Next Door' it was called. I loved that book. If we mucked up he wouldn't read it to us, that sort of thing. His name was Mr Williams and he had come from the war. He was an incredible person.

In his book, my step brother Mick describes my Grandmother Lavalle. He says she knew everything that was going on and was known to everyone as "Queen of the Loo". He also says she was 'not to be crossed'. We copped it a bit with her. She had no legs, I remember first one leg, then none, from diabetes, but she was a very big woman and the hallway was narrow so you couldn't get past her without her landing a couple of thumps. Her daughter was starting to have kids and it was only a small house so it was a matter of unloading someone – and I was the likely one to get pushed back where I came from. I had been there a year and a half when my grandmother sent me back to Kiama to live with my step mother once again.

It was the same as before, she was very strange. Tea was at 4.30 in the afternoon, then we had to go to bed. When she wanted visitors to go she would say 'I think your car is ready to go'. She is passed away now. There are many stories about my step mother. I am very polite about her in comparison to what my brothers say. I think the best story however is about my brother Joe. We were never allowed to eat the peaches even when they fell off the tree so when she wasn't looking Joe climbed up and ate the other side of every peach, the side you couldn't see. At least we got a laugh out of that.

Better off with Daisey

My sister Daisey stayed on with Grandmother Lavalle. She wasn't treated very well. Her value was to clean the house and be an interpreter; that was about it. Daisey married at 16 years of age to Frank Pirrello and I went and lived with them in Nicholson Street, Woolloomooloo. I am ever thankful to Daisey, and to Frank. I went to Plunkett Street Primary School while I was there, and in the afternoons I got a job at the paper shop on the corner. I was delivering newspapers to places in the Domain and Macquarie Chair and also to two hotels on the waterfront. Daisey and Frank had very little money. My bed was newspapers on springs so I was saving up for a mattress. I would give my pay to my sister every week. Life was interesting to say the least as Woolloomooloo was really a world of its own – there wasn't anything that didn't go on there. The guys in the pubs were wharfies, big guys who loaded huge bails of wool or they worked on the trawlers. Guys working on trawlers were usually trying to get away from something. On the boats they could keep out of sight of the police for a couple of weeks. They were a tough looking bunch but they gave me tips, especially at one hotel called the 'Rock and Roll'. I got my best tips when the 'GIRL' would walk up and down on the bar. One guy would give me two shillings for a newspaper that cost sixpence and tell me to keep the change. He was distracted – too busy looking at the 'GIRL' and at his ticket to see if his number was called. I was about ten years old and never really understood what was going on but I certainly did later.

Daisey did not like my friends from school – they were always getting up to no good. She was looking out for me and endeavoring to keep me in line. Sometimes I would come home with a comic and she would start hitting me saying I stole it. I didn't know how she knew, until later when I found out the comic had a date in the top corner and it was the next edition to be released into the shops.

Hotels in those days had a door from the footpath that led down to the cellar. Barrels of beer would be unloaded here. I remember, if the door was open and I was with my friends, one of us would jump down through the door and hand us up an empty quarts beer bottle each. We took them to the front bar where the barman would give us a shilling for each one. We would all then run off and buy an ice cream for three pence (a real treat I can tell you) and laugh all the way home. I never told my sister.

While I was in Sydney with Daisey I went prawning with my brother-in-law in Sydney Harbour. We went on weekends and all through school holidays. I didn't know how important that experience of going prawning with Frank would later become for me!

I never got the mattress. My father wanted me back in Kiama. He had bought a fish and chip shop and wanted me to work out the back. I had to leave Daisey's. She had been really great, she was the only support I actually had and we got along fine. We still get along fine.

Out on my own

Before I turned thirteen I was kicked out once again. I was about half way through primary school when my step mother put me on a fish truck that was going to Ulladulla. A lot of the relatives lived there. I began working for my two older brothers – Joe was 17 years old and Micky 21 years old – fish trawling on the *St Michele*. I didn't go to school again. They paid me £5 a week. Board was £3 a week so it was not a good deal. It didn't last for long. Three brothers and a brother-in-law working together did not work out. We argued all the time.

They each told me a different thing to do at the same time, I just couldn't handle it, I couldn't be in that many places at once.

When I was fifteen years old I left working for my brothers and started work with Davey Dunn. It was my first really good job where I was appreciated. We worked his 45 foot boat two-handed. He had called it *Battle-Axe* after his mother-in-law. Pay scales in those days were different. There was a married man's rate and a single man's rate. I was only fifteen yet he gave me a married man's rate. So I must have been OK. There were a lot of boats out there then, about eighteen, with three or four on each boat and I had the best deck-hand job in town. After tax I was clearing £16.10 a week, a substantial wage. I should have stayed with him. Instead I listened to my brother Tory when he talked me into going to work with him in Sydney.

While I was with Davey Dunn, times were good and we had had some good adventures. One trip we were going way up north. It was a holiday for Davey and I went along to steer the boat, so it was a paid holiday for me. Not long into the trip we could see a cyclone coming and we had to take shelter for a whole week. We pulled in at Evans Head. I got to know Bully (Keith Elkerton), another deck-hand at the time. Bully is a year older than me and we became life-long friends. Over the years our families have spent a lot of time together. Regrettably his wife Joan passed away but I still have a good catch up with Bully on the phone on a regular basis. I got my driver's licence at 16 and saved enough to buy my first car – a 1950 Holden. It cost me £520.

Meeting Jenny

I had also met my first wife, Jenny Mison, I met her before I was fifteen, and by sixteen I had asked her to marry me. Things were looking very good and I should have stayed working in Ulladulla, where Jenny was.

The plan with my brother Tory was to work with him at 'Hill's Hoist' in Sydney. In no time I could own a truck like he did. It sounded good but I really burnt my bridges, it took me years to get over that. Tory's grand plan was all shit – instead of getting to own a truck I lost my car, slept on a couch for a year and was too ashamed to go back to Ulladulla. My relatives would certainly have had an opinion. When Tory and his family moved from Sydney to Canberra for work I felt I had to move there too. I worked at anything, from delivering coal to working in the pine forest. Jenny and I stayed in touch and commuted backwards and forwards.

When I was eighteen and living in Canberra my father contacted me to say he was retiring from fishing. He had a proposition to put to me. He wanted me to come back to Kiama to skipper his boat, the *San Antonio*, and to work with my younger step brother Sam. It was a way back for me and I accepted his offer. No one said anything at the time but just about everyone told me later that they knew it would not work out.

Once again I was living in Kiama. Jenny and I were married and we had our own home in Minnamurra Street. I had met Jenny years before, at the Ulladulla pool, a sea pool where everybody meets – and from that time on she was my long-term girlfriend. I remember how she desperately wanted a tan like mine but could only get herself sunburnt. We really clicked together nicely, we could talk and we understood each other. Jenny was an incredible girl having her own problems in her family, so in many ways it suited us both to get married. My new wife had to get a job so we could pay off our little house so she got a job in Wollongong in the Berlei factory. Wollongong is 25 miles from Kiama and all the girls would put in for petrol and travel together. It was hard factory work, like it was in those days, with various groups of workers trying to control the place. Berlei were making bras and sports jackets and Jenny was very good at it. She soon decided her old sewing machine at home was far too slow so we bought an industrial one for her. She could really make that thing go.

Jenny's parents, Charlie and Lyn, were a great help to us both. They helped us buy the house in Minnamurra Street and later our first boat, a 32 foot fishing vessel the *Maluka*. We loved that boat. We paid them back when we sold the house and over the years we were fortunate to be able to repay their kindnesses to us. We took them on holidays overseas and to Perth with us when I was sailing in the Australian Championship, and we always enjoyed their company.

Sadly, it did not work out in Kiama. Fishing in and around Kiama was never all that good, you had to travel a long way up and down the coast, so there was not a lot of money, and it was not good with Dad and the 'old girl' (my step mother) either. The family were right, no one could work with my father with my step

MALUKA — ULLADULLA
Owner: Bartolomeo(Bob)Puglisi
Approximately 1962

mother around – somehow or other she would always muck it up. Everyone was very critical of what we had tried to do.

We decided to get out, to sell the house and to move back to Ulladulla. We bought a block of land in Jubilee Avenue and turned a shed at the back of it into a flat. I worked on that and on a local trawler while we waited for the house in Kiama to sell. As there was not town water, only rain water I dug a well with just a spade. An old man came with his dousing sticks and told me where to dig. The hole ended up so deep I almost couldn't get out!

Looking after both homes was hard work and a costly exercise as well. When the house at Kiama sold we bought the *Maluka*, a trap and long line boat, and I could work it by yourself. I had twelve fish traps and several long lines. I was so proud of my first little boat and to my surprise one morning, a few years later, I found a note on board. It was from a visiting senior constable, and came with some equipment he thought I might like. I had talked with him a few times, he used to come for holidays, but I had no idea he was a policeman.

Opposite: Pulling alongside a larger boat, my first little boat the *Maluka* at Ulladulla, New South Wales.

Drummoyne Police Station.
9th March 1964.

Dear BOB.

You dont known me personally, but I am an ardent admirer of you and your little boat, you might recall I was on the Jetty last month when you returned from fishing and I complemented you for the ship shape way you keep your boat. You have a beautiful little boat and it is a credit to you. I have been associated with fishing all my life and I must say that you are the tidxiest fisherman I have ever seen.

Bob these are a few slings I have had around for a long time, I thought perhaps you may be able to use them for mooring lines.

Your sincere admirer.
Lloyd. Shipton.
Senior/Constab le.

I have kept this letter a long time. It is important to me. I still have a reputation for keeping a boat tidy and scrupulously maintained. I just think it is easier to make sure nothing goes wrong, than to have problems and have to stop and waste time fixing them.

In 1963 our first daughter, Angelina, was born. We were living in the flat at the time. She was a lovely child and always a bit of a character. She loved the boat and fishing and would have made a great fisherwoman, however from the start it was obvious that Angelina would be a performer. Her favourite song was 'Hey Big Spender' when she was only small! As she grew up she would invite her friends around, I would make a stage and they all had a sing along. At 14 years of age Angelina performed in Port Lincoln's 'Tunarama' Festival. It was for a rock concert at the Port Lincoln Town Hall and she sang in front of 700 people. She has made a life for herself in New South Wales as a professional musician, playing the piano and singing. She is also in a three-piece band, playing in various clubs and venues.

She loves this life and would be happy doing gigs every night of the week. We have had to encourage her to scale back and take on teaching as she is getting older; we have helped her with a house with a verandah as a waiting room and a music room for lessons. She teaches singing and piano and other instruments to people of all ages. She's a good teacher, great with kids. Angelina has worked very hard getting into the music business, went to University and so on. In the early days she would get so mad with her brother as he worked only two weeks prior to a piano exam and passed. Angelina worked really hard all year to pass. She kept at it and has done so well, she has always been a clever girl. When she visits she still likes to fish off the boat. If she doesn't get a bite she says "Dad, I am sure its better over there. Can we move over there right now?"!

When naming Angelina, and all of our children, we went against the Italian tradition and called them what we liked. We were the first in the family to do so and the oldies frowned on us, but we got over that one. Am I still happy we did this? Oh yeah. In Ulladulla especially, there are just too many families with the name 'Puglisi' and it gave us huge problems. Joe Puglisi's and Tory's and Mick's were everywhere. When it came to getting mail my letters would almost always go to another Puglisi first. My uncle, he lived down the street a bit, he had twelve kids; another uncle down the hill a bit further he had five – all Puglisi's and that's just in the one street! One time by the time I got my letter I only had 14 days to pay or go to jail. So around 1962 I fixed that problem, I formed a company 'Kinkawooka Pty Ltd'. From that time onwards I received all my mail direct! We thought a lot about the name. We had bought a block of land out from Ulladulla at Cockwhy Creek. It was degraded, the trees had been cleared, so it looked rough, but it was inside a loop of the creek with water on three sides. We chose the name 'Kinkawooka' as it meant 'good waters' or 'plentiful waters' in the Aboriginal dialect. I have kept this company name all these years. The logo now has the first freezer boat I owned, the prawn, the tuna the mussel and a map of half Australia, the half that I have fished.

My step brother Mick and brother Joe were still fishing together. Dad had sold them his war-time boat the *St Michele* and they had taken it to try fishing in South Australia. They converted the old trawler for tuna fishing and moved to Port Lincoln. At the end of each tuna season in South Australia they came back for the New South Wales tuna season, so we kept up that way. Communication was difficult otherwise, as radio contact was poor.

One time though I was anchored off Bateman's Bay. It was 31 March 1965 and I could hear the radio as clear as clear. It was early morning and no one else was talking yet so reception was good. A message came through that the *St Michele* had crashed into Neptune Island in South Australian waters. Other boats were nearby and looking to see if my brothers Mick and Joe and the rest of the crew were all right. Others started talking and I lost reception, not really knowing if they were OK. I picked up my anchor straight away and after three and a half hours I was back in Ulladulla. Nolly was working at the co-op at the end of the jetty so I told her the message and she started ringing around to find out what was going on. They all had survived. What was left of the *St Michele* had leaned on the rocks and they could jump off. Mick ended up in the water when the boat pulled away and Joe threw him a rope. The reason the boat was wrecked was that the guy supposed to be steering fell asleep. The rule is to wake the owners, in this case Micky and Joe, an hour before an island is close so the owners can guide it safely through. He was asleep and it just kept going.

I had sold my little boat, I had wanted to move up in the world to a prawn trawler so I got one built in Ballina at Barlow's shipyard. We named her *Angelina Star*. She was a 45 footer. It took until the following year for her to be finished so I worked for Joe Campisi on his boat the *Aroaria* while my boat was being built. We checked on *Angelina Star* a number of times while she was being built and got to like Ballina. We could see potential for prawns there if you worked very hard. Other types of fishing seemed good too so we decided to move there. With only four serious owner / operators in Ballina, and with my experience in prawning I felt I had an edge. There were other prawn boats too, investment boats with paid staff, but these weren't serious competition. The men knocked off with their cheques and just laid them on the bar at the pub until they were gone. I would go fishing with Bully instead. He knew a lot about fishing and I learnt as much as I could from him.

About this time Jenny and I went guarantor to help Frank and Daisey buy a boat the *Rhonda*. There might have been some pressure from the family to help, I can't really remember, but actually I was happy to help Daisey and Frank for when I was little and they helped me survive. It was a bit silly as I then had to have my mother-in-law go guarantor for us, but it worked out fine and I felt it was an opportunity to pay back Daisey and Frank in some way.

I began to do well and at the time my deckhand Herby who was an interesting character kept us entertained. He sang and played the guitar some nights in the local pubs and the day after would come down to the wharf really happy and singing but late for work. I got really mad with him as I hated that the other boats had left already and got to the best spots, so one day I said "Herby you should stop fishing and go just into entertaining all the time". He did and years later I saw him on TV. It could have been one of the first 'Australia's got Talent' shows. He played a gum leaf and my memory is he came second. It was so good to see him again.

Our second child Andrew was born in 1967 while we were still in Ballina. When Andrew was small he loved going down to the boat with me. This also gave Jenny a break. When we came to Port Lincoln he would come with me on the boat in the daytime while we tested our prawn gear in Boston Bay. He always wanted to help the boys (crew) on deck. He would come into the wheelhouse and say the boys washed over the side the crabs he was keeping. Andrew today is still involved in the fishing industry. His thing is mussels and he does well. It is a difficult industry, a low price product with slim margins, but he likes working all that out so now he has all he needs to make it work.

I remember once when I was home from fishing and Jenny was busy in the kitchen making cakes for school. Andrew and I quietly operated on a ring cake whilst Jenny was out of the room, removing a couple of slices and then did the icing repairs. We thought she would not notice the reduced size – how wrong we were. I still have a laugh about it today and have often told the story to different friends.

Andrew has stayed living in Port Lincoln, he married Kristina Ricov and they have three children, Maya, Beau and Sonny. He has fished in other States as well as South Australia and has studied in Tasmania for his tickets, but his home is Port Lincoln where he has been since he was one.

When we were still in Ballina with our two small children we realised we were doing well – we were three months ahead in our bank repayments. It was all about working hard and putting in the time. We started talking and decided to move somewhere else to improve ourselves. With three months up our sleeve we could do it. Our friends Bully and Brian, both owner / operators, were getting ready to move to the Gulf of Carpentaria to catch banana prawns and we decided we might go with them. We were truly keen so packed the kids in the car to travel up to see Bully and Brian in Southport. We met in Brian's house with their wives, it was Keith (Bully) and Joan Elkerton and Brian and Barbara Blanch at the meeting. All was going well, we had decided to go – when we got to the bit about where we would all live. Brian's wife Barbara had been to Karumba and suggested the caravan park, we could all live there. Then she put her foot in it, saying "It is really, really great at the caravan park now, the owners have put wire netting right around the whole park so the crocs won't eat the kids". Well, that was it. Jenny spat the dummy, she threw her hands up in the air and said "the kids and I are not bloody going". We did not go to the Gulf!

Back in Ballina we still wanted to go somewhere, just not to the Gulf of Carpentaria. My brothers Micky and Joe lived in Port Lincoln and encouraged us to join them. They started to say to us "there is prawns over here". One boat was giving it a try but it was not easy and it had had little success. Prawn trawling is not just a matter of the right gear attached to a boat. Otter boards that keep the net spread take a lot of getting used to, the net has to sweep the bottom just right so you can catch the prawns. You can't just get the gear and know what to do, it's a real balance getting the boards to work, they have to be pulled through the water just right, the right speed, the right angle, adjusting as you go, so the water can push apart the boards. The aim is to net everything inside a 20 metre strip, the trick is to use as little fuel as possible to keep the otter boards apart and maintain a speed through the water.

Port Lincoln would be a big step for us, and though my brothers were keen, we wanted to hear from someone else as well. Luckily three Port Lincoln fishermen, Mike Leech, Max Curtis and Tom Bascombe were travelling through to Queensland and my brothers suggested they drop in on me at Ballina. I took them out prawning for the night and asked them all the questions I could, discussing at length regarding some prawns they had seen in Spencer Gulf. They loved the prawns I cooked on the boat that night. Catches were only small at the time and I thought they would eat the lot! They were tuna fishermen and as part of that they netted bait at night. They used a light to attract the bait, keeping it alive by scooping it into tanks of water on deck. They had started to see that some prawns were coming up to the light as well. They told me a story they had heard in the pub of a power line across the top of Spencer Gulf. During construction the divers were coming in and saying prawns were bumping into them with their sharp spikes. They were actually piercing holes in their wetsuits. There really must have been a lot of prawns! People had mucked around with the idea of prawning for a lot of years but no one yet did it for a living. The closest commercial prawn fishery to Port Lincoln was at Lakes Entrance in Victoria. These discussions on the boat, along with encouragement from my brothers Micky and Joe, convinced us to give it a go. My son Andrew was then about eight or nine months old and Angelina five years old.

I phoned the fisherman who was already looking at prawning, Roger Hallett. I talked with him a few times and sometimes also talked to his wife, regarding me coming across to Port Lincoln. They both warned me it might not work out for me – their nets were ripping on the rough bottom of Spencer Gulf and they were not having much success. Financially things were tight for us but I sent to him a new cotton net, the sort we were using on the bad bottom we had off Ballina.

We made the decision to go and on 14 December 1967 I left Ballina for South Australia in the *Angelina Star* with my younger half brother Anthony who was also my crew member.

Two attempts to get to South Australia

At the end of the New South Wales tuna season brothers Mick and Joe were travelling back to South Australia for Christmas in their new boat the *Dinjerra*. We were to meet them in Eden and travel together. Anthony wrote the log. George, the name we gave to our automatic pilot, features in this first entry:

'Angelina Star'
December 14 1967, Thursday … Crossed Ballina bar at – 17:35. Slight swell on bar no breaking waves. Waved farewell to Jen … all is well … George is working very well praying he doesn't get sick otherwise there will be many long hours spent at the weel. Only had light tea baked leg lamb sandwiches.

By 17 December we met our brothers and departed Eden, the larger *Dinjerra* in front of the *Angelina Star*, laden with 44 gallon drums of extra fuel and new spare trawl boards strapped on deck. Mick and Joe expected a change in the weather, even gale force, but thought it wouldn't be too bad and we could shelter in behind the 'prom'. The wind hit us with a thud. We were two thirds of the way to Wilson's Promontory, about twelve hours from Eden, when we got caught in very, very, very bad weather. It is the worst weather I have seen. It really was extremely frightening – it just got wilder and wilder, I think the wind was 70 to 80 miles per hour. For years after I got tensed up when I talked about it and I hate thinking about it even now – I often change the subject when I am asked about that first trip. My boat was actually doing well, better than the *Dinjerra* – parts of their wheelhouse and the big glass spray shield had busted away, they were having a lot of problems there. The waves were massive, unbelievably massive, but it was the curl on the wave that got me in the end. We were going right up each huge wave then right down and all waves have a curl on the top of them but these curls came way over on top of my boat and just dropped in on top of us. I had to quickly decide what to do and we all turned back. The closest place to go was all the way back to Eden, we had cut across in a straight line for Wilson's Prom so we were way out at sea and nowhere was any closer. Anthony wrote of the experience on the way back. He recalled watching the *Dinjerra*:

> I watched her hit one steep wall which was easy 30 feet from the bottom of the trough to the tip of the wave she completely disappeared in spray and white water that happened a few times but that one I took special notice of … that wave I hope if I ever see again it will be [when I am on a very big boat, say 50,000 ton] then I won't mind that special wave … if the Dinjerra never broke it [for us] I wouldn't be writing this log now.

Back at Eden Mick heard on the radio that Adelaide was not giving out any licences, they would not let me fish for prawns in South Australia. I was not happy. I had had it by then, so I said "Righto I'm going home". I headed north and pulled in at Newcastle where the police let me tie up at their wharf. We walked to the station just across the way and caught the train the rest of the way to Ballina for Christmas. You can imagine Jenny!

Back home I received a phone call. It was from Dick Fowler, head of SAFCOL (the South Australian Fishermen's Co-Operative Ltd). He had also talked to Mick and Joe and said the government had OK'd it for me to fish for prawns in South Australia. He had checked and clarified with the government authorities. He would also have a house for us in Port Lincoln, he said. He could see I had potential and from his business point of view he thought that an extra fishery would do them a lot of good. He was really keen to help.

Well, that put me in an awkward position. Not only did I have to be keen again myself, but I had to convince Jenny. She got extremely worried about how bad the weather might be in South Australia. I made silly promises about fishing behind islands but she could see through all that. It was a huge gamble but my brother Anthony and I once again headed off in *Angelina Star* – from the police wharf in Newcastle on to Ulladulla, Eden, Portland and Port Lincoln. It was an uneventful trip.

The weather we had experienced on that first attempt doesn't happen very often. It is highly unusual and catastrophic. Mick had certainly never seen weather like this before. The day we turned back on that first attempt, Harold Holt, Prime Minister of Australia, disappeared in wild seas at Cheviot Beach. He was further along the coast, past Wilson's 'Prom', but it was the same weather that had got us. Years later, in 1998, this same sort of weather system hit again in the same area. It was the year all those boats got lost in the Sydney to Hobart Yacht Race. Five yachts sank, six lives were lost and numerous helicopter rescues were made. No wonder I still shudder at those memories.

Early days in Port Lincoln – the beginnings of a prawn industry

When we finally arrived Port Lincoln seemed such a small isolated place. I joked with my brothers that "I can't see any kangaroos hopping in the streets". We met straight away with Roger Hallett who I had talked with on the phone. He was a crayfisherman working the *Cape Baron* in Port Lincoln and he was trying to establish that there might be a prawn industry in South Australia. After some chatting I was surprised to learn he had not tried the net I had sent him. I was dismayed as it had cost nearly the last bit of money we had, but I think really he just had no knowledge of how to set it up – I had given him directions but there was no-one in Port Lincoln to actually show him how.

Dick Fowler was true to his word. He provided us with a house and helped us in every way. He was a big operator in the industry and wanted to see if we could make a go of it. When there had been opposition from the older established fishermen not wanting us eastern state fishermen coming into their South Australian waters (the reason, my brothers had been told, that my licence was denied), Dick Fowler had squared it for us. There was still opposition but with the help of Dick Fowler, and others, we got through. We simply kept on with what we were doing, we were very busy, and tried not to cause ripples. Mick and Joe had had it easier when they first come across – they came just as one boat in a big tuna fleet so they hadn't struck such opposition. They were by now quite settled – and it was good that they were here.

I flew back to Ballina for Jenny and the kids. The Morris 1100 was absolutely packed to the hilt. In those days we made the back seat flat, packing our things where your feet go, so kids could lie down and move around. Crossing the Hay Plains the heat was intense and Andrew had the mumps. I thought – no worries, we will stop at a motel in Hay, put the air conditioner on, sleep a few hours, then take off again. Well, at eleven at night we switched off the air conditioner, went outside and it was just as hot. We questioned the girl at the service station who said it had been the same for a month. She had been to a place called Wollongong, she said, but it was too cold so she came back.

We squeezed ourselves back in the car and kept going. Jenny kept asking "How much further?". She didn't forgive me for ten years for 'bringing her over here to Port Lincoln'.

My first trip out prawning was on 14 January 1968. I trawled in an area called 'the gutter' off Cowell where Roger Hallett had tried before. The gutter is a natural trough in the floor of the gulf, where the bottom is reasonably smooth. Anthony and I did well, pulling up about 1500lbs of prawns over two nights. This was better than our catches in Ballina! I had only single gear (one net on the bottom) and wished there were other boats doing the same. It helps to have boats in different spots to guage the best place.

Unfortunately we broke an axle on the winch and had to return to Port Lincoln instead of slipping quietly into Cowell to unload. It was daytime by then and I think the whole of Port Lincoln saw us coming and came down to the wharf to see what we had caught. Three months later, on 14 April 1968, an article came out in the Port Lincoln Times:

Sensational Catches Excite Fish Industry … Tuna boats join prawn 'gold rush' … Sensationally valuable catches of prawns being unloaded at Port Lincoln and a slump in the tuna season could lead to a rapid development of a prawn fishery – a new industry – in Port Lincoln. … Several tuna boats are switching to prawn fishing following the landing of bonanza prawn catches at Port Lincoln which indicate the sensational potential of the industry, being pioneered at present by only a couple of boats … Two Port Lincoln boats, the *Cape Baron* and *Angelina Star*, are believed to be landing about 8000 lbs. of prawns a week between them. In a fabulous haul on the weekend the two local boats are believed to have caught 6000lbs. of prawns between them in one night's fishing. The fishermen are paid 65c. a lb. for the prawns, which are cooked on board the boats and are frozen by SAFCOL … TUNA BOATS CONVERT … It appears that many boats in Port Lincoln's tuna fleet will now convert to prawn trawling.

The *Angelina Star* was now a 'local boat' (at least according to the local paper), which was good to hear. In the financial year 1967 – 1968 very little tuna was caught in South Australia, it was a very bad year – *Karina-G* caught only 40 tons that year. Compared to that, we were really having very good catches – 12,000 lbs. of prawns for three nights was one of our bigger catches. We took some of Mick and Joe's crew onboard for a night so they could see what to do when they too started prawning in the Spencer Gulf with the *Dinjerra*.

The high was short-lived. All of a sudden Mick Olsen, Director of Fisheries, closed down prawn fishing in South Australia for two weeks and told us (Joe, Mick and myself) to come to Adelaide for a meeting. I have to say I was shitting myself. At the meeting Mick Olsen thumped the table. "Look you guys" he said, "I don't want this new fishery to stuff up like it did in the east, so what do I do, I want your advice." He knew that fisheries in the eastern states were completely out of control and over fished. With our experience coming from the eastern states, Olsen was looking for comments from us to help him not allow the same problems to occur in South Australia. I talked about 2 inch mesh and a total number of boats. He said "About 24 prawn boats and licences" and I said "That's good". It was a big job Mick Olsen was doing, he was on his own really with lots of pressure from certain quarters to just catch whatever was there and as much as possible. What Mick Olsen did was very important – a lot of things that happened then are still in place today. He hasn't been recognised enough.

Jenny got to like Port Lincoln, especially after she worked out how to grow vegetables in the local climate. We bought a house in Easton Road. I remember when Jenny found it. I was out on the water. Safcol had a system where they radioed to check each boat morning and night. It was usually a quick affair – "*Angelina Star* OK?" and my reply "*Angelina Star* OK". On this day – "Message for *Angelina Star*, call home as soon as possible". I was near Walleroo where there was a phone on the jetty. Jenny was waiting for my call – "You have to come home, you have to come home right now". There was a house for sale and she definitely wanted it, she did not want to miss out. I was relieved the kids were safe and just said OK.

Jenny was really great. She did a lot in the community, established a library at the Catholic School, set up a second hand uniform shop with other parents. She worked in that shop for many years.

In 1969, our third child, Carmel, was born – the only one of our three children to be born in Port Lincoln. Carmel was a bugger of a child, I still tell her that. Each day she would be last to do her piano practice and delay it until it was time to go to school, then it was little practice or none at all. She had it easier than the older ones of course and she was a smart cookie so she could work the fact that she was the youngest. She was hard work with her eating. I remember she was made to sit at the table many times until she had finished her dinner. She would often sit and scrape the fat off her grilled whiting!!! Sometimes when Jenny and I went away for a break her Grandma Bowden came across to look after the children. Her grandma let Carmel eat just about anything she wanted and that was lots of ice cream. I still hear my daughter talk about her problems with food and she still talks fondly of her grandma. Carmel went on to be a nurse and still is a practicing nurse in New South Wales. She married Peter Sumich and has two boys Jay and Will.

Late in 1969 I went to Ballina Slipway and ordered a new prawn trawler, a 64'6" steel boat that I also called *Angelina Star*. It was time to up-grade. I sold my old *Angelina Star* to Hagen Stehr.

Within a short time 34 prawn licences were issued – a lot more than originally planned. Mick Olsen resisted huge pressure as well as threats. People just wanted to move into prawning. With tuna so scarce they needed the money, so they had to do something, but it wasn't good. They would show a few receipts to say their boats were converted when really they weren't. Mick Olsen regrettably left the department and the next Director of Fisheries didn't have a clue. We still have about five too many licences in the industry.

Australian Bight Fisheries – expansion on the world market

I was still using SAFCOL to process the prawns that we caught. They were kept in brine on the boat and covered with ice to keep out the air, then brought in for processing. We were all starting to think we were not getting a fair price for our product, so Mick suggested all the fishermen start a processing works ourselves. In 1970 I was one of twelve boat owners that formed a company called 'Australian Bight Fisheries Pty Ltd', a company that would process our prawns so we could get a fair price. It became a huge venture. I did marketing and research on behalf of 'Bight', employing a skipper when needed for *Angelina Star*. In the mid – 1970s I travelled to Malaysia three times – as a director of Australian Bight Fisheries I was involved in setting up prawn processing there. I travelled to Japan and South Africa regarding the sale of prawns, and to visit customers. Also to Darwin as prawns from there were being processed by us; to Canberra to try to get my brother Tory to sell prawns for 'Bight' in ACT; and to Melbourne to look for a scallop boat to survey our waters to investigate the possibility of a scallop industry. The town was desperate to create new fishing industries because tuna catches were still very low. I later went to Japan, twice, regarding the sale of tuna.

Working with 'Bight' was good as I was having the opportunity to get off the boat and employ skippers instead. This gave me the opportunity to travel for 'Bight' but also time to run the business, make nets, and have time to be home with the family. You blink three times and kids are not so little anymore. I loved fishing and travelling but when I was away I always felt I was missing out.

The processing works was a boom for the town, employing a lot of local people especially women. Women seemed more careful at grading the prawns but it was an awful job. We eventually bought a peeling machine which cut the number of women needed to peel prawns. They didn't mind – no more swollen hands and they all still had jobs in other parts of the factory. We always moved them around to different jobs to keep work interesting for them.

I sold my steel *Angelina Star* to my brothers Mick and Joe and took ownership of a new boat. I wanted a more versatile vessel, one that I could use for prawning, fish trawling and for tuna fishing. My new *Angelina* was built in Adelaide and she stayed prawning until 1978, when I switched her to fish trawling instead – in South Australia, Victoria and New South Wales.

We were doing well with our new *Angelina* so after two years with her I was able to help Daisey and Frank once again. Around 1974 I loaned them the deposit of $10,000. for a fish trawler which cost $70,000. and they did so well with it they managed to pay me back in just two years. Daisey is still special to me; she is still the same. Life isn't easy for her since Frank has passed away but she still smiles – and she still wants to know everything that is going on.

In 1976 Jenny and I sold our home in Easton Road and this time bought an old house, built in 1908, in Prospect Road, Port Lincoln. Angelina was by now thirteen, Andrew nine and Carmel seven. The kids have had a good time here, bringing all their friends around. Over the years we restored and renovated the old home and I still live in her with my new wife Musharella. And we are still renovating. It's a nice old house and, because of its size and the amount of land around us, it is very easy to live in.

When I switched the new *Angelina* to fish trawling I was away a lot. Still with 'Bight' I was now catching different types of fish but further afield. We had a huge haul of gem and mirror dory that we unloaded in Sydney Harbour so we sent it back to Bight in two semi-trailers to be processed. We then fished off Portland on the way home. 'Bight' now owned David Hyland Fisheries processing factory as well, so all those eastern states fish we set back for processing which kept the processing factory going well. The David Hyland

Fisheries processing factory was then located opposite the silos where the TAFE college is and it was busy all the time. It was a very successful time for us and having a boat that we could switch from prawn trawling to fish trawling really paid off.

After we unloaded our catch from that huge trip we went out again to experiment with fish trawling south of Neptune Island and off the continental shelf. The plan was to survey for five days but a gearbox problem saw the survey abandoned.

The next experiment came to nothing as well. I was waiting for my next boat, a 66 foot prawn trawler, to be built when I had the opportunity to skipper the *Jeanette*, a 48 foot Danish Seiner (pronounced sayna) belonging to my Uncle Sam. I wanted to try out Danish Seining in South Australia, a method of fishing used in many parts of the world. A specially shaped weighted net is carefully placed on the sea floor then wing nets pulled forward to surround the fish and herd them into the net. The South Australian Department of Fisheries set the conditions of the trial. I was to personally be on board and information on all trawl shots was to be submitted to the department. We surveyed from Kangaroo Island to Cape Radstock, from 16 fathoms to the continental shelf, trawling the seabed for fish. It was worth a try but in the end catches were poor.

I was still waiting for my boat so went to Sydney to help my step father-in-law Joe Bowden fit out his fish trawler the *Beaver*. After three weeks of hard work he offered to fly me back in his twin Comanche aeroplane. This sounded good to me and for a while it was. We were chatting about this and that and coming near to Port

Lincoln airport when Joe seemed to be trying to get open a little hatch between the seats. I said to him "What is wrong Joe?" and he said "The light to show the wheels are down is not coming on. There is a handle under the hatch cover to pump the wheels down". I said to him "Joe just fly the plane, I will pump the wheels down" and you bet I did this super fast. We flew right over the airport and even over Coffins Bay or somewhere. We landed safely after a while and I can't remember ever flying with him again.

I ended up buying the *Beaver* and Anthony fish trawled with it out of Sydney for a while. After a time he brought it round to Port Lincoln where we re-built it for prawns. I sold the *Angelina*, went prawning in the *Beaver*, then sold it to a fisherman in Venus Bay. So many boats, but not confusing to me, I know them all. With every boat there is a new purpose or a new improvement, allowing less and less days on the water to fill our quota for the same return, freeing up time to be employed in other ways. The next *Angelina*, a freezer boat, was built in Queensland, at Jaden's on the Gold Coast. It was the second freezer prawn trawler in South Australia.

In 1982 I left Australian Bight Fisheries. It was no longer really helping me, so I left the company and went about selling my own product again. For me there was no real need for a processing facility. Because I had a freezer boat I only needed a buyer. Prawns can be frozen and sold in bulk, leaving the buyer to process or sell. On later boats I have basically put a factory onboard. Prawns land, pass through a grader to sort them by size, are cooked if need be, then packed and frozen in cardboard boxes. When you open such a box and thaw it in water it is the freshest product you can possibly have.

Being part of Australian Bight Fisheries was good for a lot of years. A lot of people in the town were employed there. But in the end it was not for me, I am not really good at working with the public in helping run a factory; I am much better with crews. 'Bight' did a lot of good things though and tried hard to introduce new products to benefit the town.

After my involvement in 'Bight' there was a sobering lull. My father passed away, I tried a new venture in the Gulf of Carpentaria, I failed in another venture with my brother Tory and a scallop survey came to nothing. But before the lull it was 1983, the year Australia won the America's Cup. The skipper was a good friend so of course we were all excited. Competitive sailing was a passion of mine and for a few years I owned and sailed some lovely yachts. We were always involved in the Soling sailing championships and one year Port Lincoln was the host. John Bertrand, his wife Rasa and their family were selected to stay with us. A long friendship developed. John loved my Jenny's homemade tomato sauce and never left empty handed. Each time he visited Port Lincoln Jenny always had a couple of bottles on hand for him to take home.

Just a few years later my Dad, Guiseppe Puglisi, passed away at the age of 84. I was in Japan at the time. When my father was 18 years old in 1920 he introduced 'set lining' for snapper into Australia. He was sent out to Australia by his family, to make good and then send back for them and their friends. It was a great responsibility as their future was put in his hands. In his one small suitcase, with very little else, he had brought with him a single set line, a long length of line with hooks set along it. He was an expert at placing the hooks along the bottom of the sea. With this single line he introduced a new method of ocean fishing along the New South Wales coast, where previously fishermen had fished only the rivers and outlets. Puglisi fishing families became famous in towns all along the coast. His contribution was just enormous. I don't think he paid enough attention to his immediate family but his contribution to the Italian community was extraordinary. To get enough money to buy a house and set it up for his father and uncle and then to get enough to bring out the rest of the family, as well as many relatives and friends, was really something. He didn't get enough appreciation for that. He had come here on his own, had got some independence in this new country, then was expected to tuck in behind his father when he arrived. There should have been more flexibility than that, but that was how it was.

I decided to expand into Queensland so I bought the *Nino*, a 65 foot freezer boat. It was licenced to fish in Queensland, the Torres Strait and Gulf of Carpentaria. I had a skipper for nine months a year and around the beginning of January each year I arrived to do maintenance which took about another month. Meanwhile I tried my hand at a new venture, going into partnership with my brother Tory and his son-in-law Randal McFie.

Together we bought 16,000 acres of land between Canberra and Cooma to spit into 40 acre blocks. It seemed a good idea as it was only a one-hour drive to Canberra and would likely be popular. The land was full of dead trees, wood that could be sold as firewood as an income while we set up all the blocks. Unfortunately a large bushfire went through and burnt the lot, so that was the end of the firewood plan. After that my brother's style of running things and mine differed too greatly and he asked if I wanted out. As I owned

50% of the land and company, and it was not working out for me, I said yes. It seems that whenever I get tangled up with relatives I get into trouble, it has taught me to be cautious once again. The whole idea was OK but it was not for me. It did not work out well for Tory and Randal in the end either.

I went back to the water, teaming up with 'Bight' again to investigate the possibility of a scallop industry in South Australia. Together we hired a top scallop fishermen, Mr John Cull from Melbourne, with his vessel the *Trinity* and we met up at Kingscote, Kangaroo Island to begin the survey. Starting on 6 January 1987 we surveyed right through to Streaky Bay, but the result was disappointing. There was not enough for commercial quantities of scallops at that time. It is always a disappointment when ventures don't work out, as they are always gone into with good intentions that they will work out really well for everyone.

Tragedy at home

It was 1990 and I had just sold the *Nino* in Queensland. I received the bad news that my wife had asbestos mesothelioma. This was very hard for the family. Jenny sadly passed away three years later (February 1994). Our children were now in their 20s. Angelina and Carmel were living and working in Sydney and Andrew was married and living and working in Port Lincoln. I was on my own and felt lost as my heart was broken. The only way I knew to get through the days and nights was to work and keep busy.

We never did figure out how Jenny got this dreadful disease. I knew as much about Jenny as she knew about herself and neither of us could think of a time she could have got it. We found out that about a quarter of people diagnosed never can pinpoint the cause. It started with Jenny not being able to catch her breath and she soon became very ill. We moved to Adelaide for nearly the whole time, we had a unit in Adelaide, and ran the boats from there. We tried everything and worked with – the Cancer Council, her medical specialists and doctors, she did meditation and also alternative therapies. Her friend Pat was very good and came to Adelaide quite a few times to look after her. We also came back to Port Lincoln at times. With kids visiting, especially at Christmases, it was much easier at home. One time coming back from Adelaide I had to drive her, as she was too ill to fly. I had her lying down in the passenger's seat as comfortable as I could get her and we could chat, but coming into Port Pirie I didn't notice I was speeding until I got pulled over by a cop. I was speeding quite a lot, I thought he would immediately take my driver's licence and I didn't know what I was I going to do to get Jenny home. But when he came over to the car and looked inside he didn't say anything for a while, then he just said "Go on, get going and slow down". I will always remember that cop. We decided to have a full-time nurse for Jenny in the day and at night we looked after her as best we could. At home we often had 'No Visitors' sign on the gate. It was devastating to lose my wife. Jenny will be long remembered. She was always involved in the Catholic school and up until recently there was a foundation in her name that I contributed to.

Tuna farming – an exciting new venture for Port Lincoln

While all this was going on with Jenny there was serious action happening with a new industry for Port Lincoln – tuna farming. Tuna had continued to be scarce in local waters but were known to be further afield. If only we could bring the tuna to Port Lincoln, feed them well and then export them. We were getting to know the Japanese market for sushi – it was huge – and the Japanese would pay lots of dollars for tuna in excellent condition. The thought was – what if we could carefully capture schools of tuna, swim them to Port Lincoln in their own time, feed them on route, then in ocean cages off Port Lincoln, continue to feed and fatten them. Tuna grow extremely quickly. Divers would help harvest the tuna out of the cages onto the deck with as little markings as possible.

First however we needed cages to tow them in, and this had never been done before. The closest we could think of were salmon cages used in Tasmania but we had no idea if they would work. It was a collaborative effort and a truly exciting one. In 1992 I went with my son Andrew to Tasmania to check out the salmon cages. It got us both away for a break from our troubles at home.

Tony Santic came as well. We checked out the salmon cage nets and especially a new system of floating plastic pipe to form the frame of the cage. Tony and I were trying to work out a way to make a cage to tow tuna and got Graham Johnson from the company to make us one to try. It was a square shape and it didn't work, it

Tuna farming in Port Lincoln – Bob Puglisi in the white coat.

Our wonderful tuna divers again.

tipped straight into the water as soon as it was towed, so we tried everything until we got it right. There were approximately seven of us, all trying to make it work – Tony Santic, Stan Lukin, Ron Forster, brother Joe, Ron Waller, Dinko Lukin and myself. It was a massive job and had not been done anywhere in the world before. Each and every day was an experience and certainly a challenge.

We tried to build up the leading edge of the cage to stop it diving beneath the water. That didn't work so we experimented with shapes. A hexagon sounded good but it collapsed, so we finally settled on a ring shape. We changed the colour as well. Black plastic tubing became too hot to work on; a change to white reduced the temperature considerably. The result is the 'tuna rings' still used today. If we carefully encircled a school, herding them into the ring, then towed the ring slowly, feeding them along the way, we could make steady progress, sometimes over hundreds of kilometres to Port Lincoln, with no panic and therefore no damage to the tuna.

The problem of course was sharks, which would bite their way in. They will try anything to get in which always damaged the net or they would get tangled up. Our divers *en route* are brave in the extreme. Working in pairs they mend the net from inside, lift and push over the edge any sharks that have got in, and from the outside, free any tangled sharks and push them back into the deep.

Once in Port Lincoln divers assist the herding of the tuna into permanent pens so officials can check the count. Once in these farms (the same sort of rings), tuna have room to grow. They swim in the same direction, clock-wise, and are fed. The occasional one that is sick will drift to the side and swim the opposite way, so is easily spotted and removed. When tuna reach the required size the divers once again go in. The way the divers handle the tuna is incredible. They grab the tail of the fish then pass each tuna up onto the deck, holding it under their gills. Within eleven seconds it is all over for the tuna. They are then immediately deep-frozen to minus 61 degrees.

As a system it works really well. Provided they have been kept stress-free and fed along the way, then looked after well in Port Lincoln, the result is a cage of fat tuna that are worth big dollars on the Japanese market.

As well as the *Angelina* I hired a tuna poling vessel the *Fina-K* and its crew – this cost me $28,000. for two weeks. On my first trip I towed 700 live tuna back to Port Lincoln, Stan Lukin towed home 650. It was a real challenge. A couple of years later I was farming 13,000 tuna, about 300 tons in 6 x 40 metre cages.

While Jenny was still alive I had purchased the *Santa Anna* and did a lot of alterations on her, new motors, bulbous bow, 1.5 m on the stern and so on. So when I started tuna farming, I had two tuna cage pens from the start – and this helped me to keep busy when I lost Jenny. I did some towing of the tuna cage pens with the *Santa Anna* and sold her around 2001. I had purchased tuna feed boats as well, the *Nina* then the *Maya*. These were to feed and generally look after the live tuna. I had three crew on each boat and later my own dive team of three. I had to buy in overseas pilchard feed because the fat content of local pilchards was low or the supply was low, but prices and supply fluctuated so I built my own freezer 400 ton capacity to store bait. Sometimes pilchards came from as far as Monteray Bay near San Francisco.

There was a lot to work out to keep the tuna healthy, especially in the early days – what to feed them, how much and how often – these calculations were critical. The quota is checked at Port Lincoln, the fish counted and the tonnage estimated – government officials do all that. After that point, it is 'added value' so the aim is to do the most you possibly can do with what you have. Feeding is all to do with colour and fat content, tailoring to the requirements of the Japanese market, and you need enough pens so they have room to grow. There were other things to think about as well. Fuel boats along with the tuna feed boats were needed to support the towing boats, and in Port Lincoln security boats were needed too, for a different kind of shark. It is disappointing but we needed boats just watching out for people who would come up to the farms, in their own boats, and steal our tuna.

When harvesting I would send some by air directly to Japan, or load onto Japanese freezer boats at the back of Boston Island. I had 20 guys working when harvesting. Days were precious, using my two prawn vessels to tow my live tuna back to Port Lincoln, meant I had to allow enough time to then get my boats ready for the prawning season that started in March.

Dealing with Japan was very interesting. I was selling in yen so had to take out forward cover in yen too. It took a lot of working out when it hadn't been done before but I thoroughly enjoyed working it out. At one point I sent four of my key staff to Tokyo for ten days for a break and to see the market operating. They all worked hard for me.

In April 1996 I received the dreaded phone call from the skipper of my tuna feed boat. Port Lincoln Bay was full of dead tuna. Overnight a mud surge, low tide and dodge tide had all occurred at the same time, depriving the tuna of oxygen. We didn't know what was happening at the time. I checked our tuna and they were getting sick but our scientific guys couldn't work out the cause. We thought they needed a feed but feeding used up more oxygen. It was a disaster. Tons and tons of tuna died – I lost 96% of my fish. Not only was it a heavy loss; it was a bad time for Port Lincoln, reeking of dead tuna for weeks, with feelings a bit raw. It was a disgusting smell, a sad smell, you didn't want them dying like that. We had to take them to the dump and streets stank with water dripping from the trucks. For weeks we were collecting dead tuna from the shore. It was a very low time and I had to wait then until the following year to start again. My quota was used up. It took a lot of getting over.

Meeting Musharella

Four months after this disastrous phone call, on the day before spring, I married my second wife, Musharella, and it was wonderful to have another soul-mate. I am the luckiest man in the world to have found two beautiful women. We have now been married for 21 years. To my deeper thoughts of amazement, as my wife

Musharella puts her creative hat on, I find out just how similar Musharella and Jenny are. They do and did such similar things and they never understand or understood boredom, there is or was always a project on the go. A fisherman or any hard working man needs a woman like this in their lives, not the type that are out on the town or at the pub all the time.

I was first aware of Musharella when my mechanic was late for work. He was helping a young lady fix her car, a Datsun Bluebird 1961, instead of being on time for me. I was cross with him of course but he was intrigued by her, so I couldn't be cross for long. Hilly and his wife already knew Musharella and he said "she would be a good catch Bob", they thought Musharella was interesting, good company and a very hard working lady.

Months later I visited my new grandchild, at their home. There was a car out the front – a Datsun Bluebird. I commented on it when a voice from the other room said "that's my car". It was Musharella, she was visiting. I plucked up the courage and said to her I would like to have a ride in that car one day! I never thought when I lost Jenny that it would happen again. It was quite a shock. After two years of marriage, Musharella left her job at the hospital behind to help me in the general running of the business, just as Jenny would have done if she had been alive today, and I thank her for that.

Musharella loves animals and we started having some fun. Tony Santic asked us if we wanted to go half shares in buying a racehorse. We called him 'Jesterella Boy' and to our surprise he won his first race, in race two on the Melbourne Cup day in 1999. We mistakenly thought we might be onto a good thing so declined a substantial offer from a well-known horse trainer. It turned out that it was a short career for 'Jesterella Boy', and for us, but Tony Santic went on to have success with the famous 'Makybe Diva' in 2003, 2004 and 2005.

We went into importing poodles instead, three red toy poodles from Texas in the United States and two toy poodles from the Netherlands, and we have had a lot of enjoyment from them. They are high maintenance with grooming etc for the shows, especially for Musharella who is the one to do most of this. Our remaining two are still a joy and a pleasure. Speaking of pleasure my other passion has been target shooting, it replaced the yachts. It fulfills a need I seem to have to be competitive and I have met some lovely people.

Other ventures

In more recent years I have built two more boats, the *Angelina* and *Beauie-J*, both steel boats, built in Adelaide. I kept these two boats and still have them. In 2003 I decided to sell the whole of the tuna farm operation – the quota, the boats, farming waters, tuna holding rings, trucks and forklifts and staff – to Tony Santic of 'Tony's Tuna'. He bought the lot, and a year later I moved into commercial mussel farming in Port Lincoln with my son Andrew.

Mussels were an interesting new venture, especially when it came to ensuring the mussels stayed fresh. We imported a special machine from Germany to vacuum pack the mussels. It cost a lot of dollars but was well worth it, essential really – as air is the enemy of mussels. It works extremely well and a pack of mussels stays alive for ten or more days. The biggest problem with mussels in Port Lincoln is the cost of freight. Melbourne has almost no freight costs and Tasmania has freight assistance and these are our main competitors. Nonetheless our product sells. The advantages of Port Lincoln are actually very important, everything is here that a fishing industry might want.

In 2009 I was talked into buying squid licences and gave squid fishing a go. We took the two freezer boats and went fishing for squid in both South Australia and Victoria but it was an absolute disaster and there was a lot of money down the drain. Squid season is right in the middle of prawn season, and prawns are what we do well, so we should have just stayed with prawning. From 2010 for the next five years I had a boat working out of Ballina with a Queensland licence, a 60 foot prawn trawler, the *New Avalon*. We had bought this boat in an effort to help family members get on their feet but it did not work out and I lost a lot of money.

In about 2011 we purchased a 58 foot steel boat for the mussel farm. We called her *Carmel*. There had been so many *Angelina*'s, and partly because *Carmel* was such a common name for boats, especially in the Croation fishing community, we had never had a *Carmel* before. I didn't realise but I did notice how pleased my daughter Carmel was to see her name on our new mussel boat. I didn't tell her it was there, I just let her see it.

In 2016 I moved out of mussels, it was mainly my son Andrew's interest more so than mine, so in exchange for Andrew's share in the prawns I transferred 'Kinkawooka Mussels', along with processing factory, licenced ocean waters, trucks, forklifts and boats *Maya* and *Carmel*. I had been shying away from it so he moved that way and grows a lot of mussels now. There have been other ventures over the years, some very short term – forestry work, buying land for units, almond growing, farming abalone, investment properties, etc – but I was always prawning right through.

Reflections

Things have changed a lot in my life but in some ways not at all. Back then there was no one to give a hug or a hand shake to. There was no one who could help us along with money in any shape or form, no one that I knew of anyway. Living with my sister Daisey and in the early years with my wife Jenny, we were all poor. To get ahead was to work and to work very hard and long days and nights and putting the time in. I can't see that that is really any different today. Today we are much more established of course, we just don't realise it. A lot is taken for granted. Now when people borrow or lend from me – equipment or money, I am lucky if I get a thank you via someone. That is just the way it is, I am not complaining. For myself though I am always respectful that someone has worked as hard as I have to give what they have given, especially if I have to borrow or lend from them. Call me old-fashioned but always when I borrow or lend from anyone I go back to them directly and thank them personally. I have always returned everything in the same order or in better condition, no matter how long it took, and I am not going to change.

I moved to Port Lincoln in 1968, 50 years ago in January, and it was my privilege to bring prawning experience with me and help establish the prawning industry here. Since 1968 I have not stopped prawning in Spencer Gulf, South Australia. It has also been great being part of establishing tuna farming in South Australia. It is such an important and exciting industry. Mussels too are now established here, and will continue.

I believe my hard work and attention to detail (someone called it 'micro-management') has paid off over the last 50 years. This – and my belief in my staff. The business is still continuing today, financially stable. Safety is at the top of my list and to this day the general up-keep and running of Kinkawooka Pty Ltd is like a clean and tidy ship. I have always believed in the hands-on approach. No one can ever successfully run a business and stay afloat if they are not there within the workings. I am proud I went this way. I have been able to help my three children greatly in establishing their businesses. I can only give them guidance now, the rest is up to them.

In the prime of my business I employed around 40 people. Now I still employ around 12. Some of my key staff have been with me 29 years, 26 years, 18 years and so on. I am very proud and they are too.

I am 75 years old now and my wife Musharella and I are going to sell the big old home of memories and she is taking me back home to Ulladulla. Port Lincoln has been good to us, a lot of headaches but a lot of good times too. It is also lovely to look at, all that water, you can never get sick of it. In going to the eastern states it will be good now to be an elder in the family, to visit whoever I want to visit and to not be told what to do. I will live out my days with family and old friends. For a time I will return to Port Lincoln in the prawning season, commuting back and forth. It is winter now and I like to see my beautiful big prawn vessels prepare once again to go to work. It is something that I still really enjoy to do.

I would like to thank Rhondda Harris and my wife Musharella Puglisi for helping me record this piece of history.

I still independently sell my prawns from my two freezer vessels from Port Lincoln.